Gigi's Bedtime Bible Stories

Stories from Scripture
adapted for children
by Jan Hadley

Drawings by Jackson Clapp,
Hadley Clapp, and Scout Caruso

Transcription, editing, and photography
by Margaret Hadley

ISBN: 9798770786330

Dedicated to all
who share their
love of God with others.

Many thanks to
REH,
PJC,
and JGH.

Contents

Preface

Dear Young Listeners and Readers,

These are Bible stories that I want to share with you, because I love God. The Bible is a book that God gave us. The stories tell us what God has done in the past and what He will do in the future. What God said is true, and experts keep finding more evidence to prove it. For example, groups of people all over the world have shared flood stories from ancient times, much like the one I'll tell you later about Noah. The Bible is my favorite book, and I hope you'll learn to love reading it, too.

Love,
Gigi

We love because God first loved us.
-I John 4:19 (GNT)

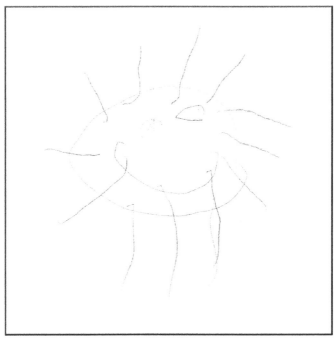

The Sun

Creation

A long, long time ago there wasn't anything, except God. He decided that He was going to say the words to create everything. He started with the heavens and earth. He separated light from darkness, then divided the waters. He made the sun, moon, and stars. He created trees and plants. After that, He made all the fish, birds, and land animals.

Then God said, "Let's make man in our own image." He took some dirt, the dust of the earth, and formed the first man. He breathed life into him, and the man was alive. Every time God had created something new, He saw that it was good. We can see that today—how beautiful the earth is, all the plants, trees, different animals, and people.

Now there was only one man, only Adam. So God said, "That's not good. Adam should have a partner, someone he can be with, who he would care for, and who could help him." While Adam was sleeping, God created Eve, the first woman.

On the seventh day, God rested.

Next God said, "I'm going to give you a job." He told the first man, Adam, to watch over the Garden of Eden and name all of the animals he saw. So that was Adam's first job.

Now Adam and Eve lived together in the beautiful garden that God had planted. Adam and Eve took care of the garden, the animals, and the trees. God would come into the garden to visit them.

That's how Creation happened. God created everything, because He has more love to give than we can imagine. He created people so that they could be His friends.

Noah

Noah and the Flood

Adam and Eve had children. Then their children had children. A long time after they lived, there were many, many people on the earth. But the people were doing very bad things. They weren't looking to God. They weren't listening to the Lord. God said, "I'm sad that I made people, because they are doing so many evil things. I know there are some good people who listen to Me, and I will protect them."

He looked around and noticed Noah. Noah was a good man. He loved God and his family. God decided that He would choose Noah to do something special. He asked Noah to build an enormous ark. An ark is a great big huge boat.

Most people didn't know about building boats, especially where Noah lived. But God told Noah, "Even though you're not living by the sea, you need to build this ark. Because I am going to send rain to cover all the earth with water, so only the people who love Me will survive."

Then Noah started building the ark. While he was working, he would talk to anyone who was around, saying, "You need to start listening to the Lord. You need to start doing what God says, because bad things are going to happen. Only the people who are inside this ark are going to be saved."

But the people around him, did they listen to him? No, they didn't. They probably even laughed at him, because they thought, *Why are you building this ark right here, where there isn't any water?*

But Noah and his family kept working. He had three sons, and each one had a wife. God told them exactly how to build the ark. They finished it.

Then God chose a male and a female—or a dad and a mom—from all the different kinds of animals to go into the ark. Every type of animal living on land or in the air was invited, because the sea creatures were just fine.

Next God said, "All right, get ready. I'll send in all the animals." The animals went inside. No other people wanted to go with them even though Noah had invited them. Noah and his family went inside the ark. Then God closed the door!

It started to rain. It was pouring, pouring rain for forty days and forty nights. That's a long, long time. Now water covered the whole earth. Then all the people who weren't listening to God, they were gone. But Noah and his family were safe, because they were inside the ark.

Noah and his family stayed inside the ark for a long time. The rain stopped after forty days, but there was still water everywhere. They had to stay inside. Noah sent out a raven, which is a big black bird, to see if there was any land for him. There was still no dry land. He waited and sent out a dove that also came back. After a couple more weeks, the dove flew out and stayed away because he found dry land. Noah and his family could finally get out of the ark!

Noah thanked God. After that, the Lord said He would never send so much rain that it would cover the earth again. God did something new. Do you know what that special thing was? He made a beautiful rainbow. Every time you see a rainbow, after it's been raining, then you can remember that God said, "I'm putting a rainbow in the sky so you'll know that I will never flood the earth again." Noah's story shows us that it's important to listen to what God wants you to do.

Stars

Abraham and Baby Isaac

A long time after Noah, there was a man named Abram. He grew up in a place called Ur, which is in Chaldea, and then lived in Haran. He and his wife Sarai lived there happily. They were old and had a lot to be thankful for. The Lord came and spoke to Abram. God said, "Abram, I have chosen you to become a great nation. I would like you, your wife, and your household to leave your home and follow Me."

Abram said, "Yes, Lord. I will do that." So they packed up, and they moved to places in Canaan that they'd never been before. The animals in their flocks grew strong and multiplied. Then they were waiting and waiting for God to tell them what to do next.

After a while, God came to Abram. The Lord said, "Abram, I'm changing your name to Abraham, because you are going to be the father of My special people. You are going to have children, grandchildren, and many great-grandchildren. I'm changing Sarai's name to Sarah, because it means princess." God made a covenant, or a promise, with Abraham. He was going to be the father of many, many people—as many as the stars in the sky. Also, God said that He's going to give these special people a land of their own.

Abraham and Sarah believed God. Sarah had never had a baby, even though she was very old. They had waited a long time—years and years—for God to give them a baby. Guess what? God came and told Abraham that it was going to happen. His wife Sarah would finally have a baby.

Not too far away, Sarah was listening. When she heard God say that, she laughed. She thought, *Oh my goodness, how can I have a baby now that I'm really old?*

But God told the truth, and in a few months Sarah had a baby boy. They called him Isaac. That was a miracle, because Abraham was almost 100 years old and Sarah was also very old. From Isaac came all the people that later we'll learn about who are called the Jews or Israelites. Today there are still Jews, God's special people, who came from Abraham through Isaac. God made a covenant with Abraham and Sarah. He kept that promise—the miracle baby Isaac. When God makes a promise, He keeps it.

Beside the Red Sea

Moses and the Exodus

After Abraham's grandson Jacob had twelve sons, there were more Israelites on the earth. God watched over them. There was a long famine, which meant the people had no food because they couldn't grow anything. So God's people moved to live in a country called Egypt, because the Egyptians had food.

The king, called the Pharaoh, became afraid of God's people, the Israelites, because there were so many of them. The Egyptians made the Israelites their slaves. Then the Pharaoh said, "Kill all the baby boys born to the Israelites."

One of God's special people, the Israelite named Moses, was born in Egypt. His mom said, "No, we can't let him be killed." His dad agreed.

Moses' mom made something pretty unusual. She lined a little basket that was kind of like a boat, and she put Baby Moses in the basket. While his big sister Miriam watched nearby, they let Moses float in the basket down the Nile River. They prayed that God would protect him.

Have you heard what God did? Pharaoh's daughter, the Egyptian princess, saw the basket with the sweet little baby boy. She said, "Oh, I'm going to take care of this baby. I'll make him my son." That's what the Pharaoh's daughter did. She raised little baby Moses. He grew up as a prince in the palace.

But Moses knew he was an Israelite. When he grew up, he saw the way that the Israelites, his people, were being treated. He got very angry. He stopped an Egyptian soldier, who was beating one of the Israelites. But Moses wasn't allowed to hurt a soldier, so Moses had to run away.

He went to live in the desert. He took care of sheep, got married, and became a daddy. He lived there for a long time—forty years. One day, he saw a bush. The bush was on fire, but it wasn't burning up. He thought, *What is that?* Moses went closer to the bush, and out of the bush came the voice of God.

The Lord said, "Do not come closer. Take off your shoes, you're in a holy place." Next God told Moses, "I'm giving you a job. I want you to go back to Egypt and tell Pharaoh to let My people go."

That's what Moses did. He went back to Egypt. All kinds of terrible things had to happen, what we call plagues. Finally, the Pharaoh said, "O.K., you and your people can go." Then Moses brought all of God's special people out of Egypt. They were walking away from Egypt—that's what Exodus means. After they left, the Pharaoh said, "Wait a minute. What did I do? I don't want to let them go. I'm going to bring them back."

Meanwhile, the Israelites came to a big body of water, called the Red Sea. They looked at it, and some thought, *How are we going to get across the Red Sea?* That wasn't bad enough! They turned and saw Pharaoh with his army coming to get them.

But guess what happened? God opened the Red Sea. He pushed the water apart, so the Israelites could cross on dry land. God held back the sea, until they got all the way to the other side.

Pharaoh and his army came. These Egyptians saw that there was dry land in the middle of the sea. They went in to get the Israelites. Do you know what God did? He put the water back. All of the Israelites were safe on the other side. But Pharaoh and his whole army were gone. They died in the water. That's another story about how God fought for His people. People who love God are protected.

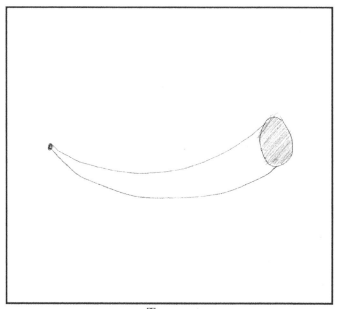
Trumpet

Joshua and Jericho

God chose Joshua to lead the Israelites after Moses died. The Israelites were traveling near Jericho. Now the city of Jericho had closed its gates. They didn't want anyone to come in.

By the city, Joshua looked up. All of a sudden, he saw a Man standing in front of him with a sword. Joshua asked Him, "Are you for us or for our enemies?"

"Neither," replied the Man, "I am the commander of the army of the Lord."

Then Joshua fell on his face to worship. Joshua asked Him, "What message does my Lord have for His servant?"

The commander of the Lord's army replied, "Take off your sandals. The place you are standing is holy." Joshua obeyed.

The Lord said to Joshua, "Listen carefully. I'm giving Jericho into your hands, along with its king and its fighting men. This is what you should do. March around the city once a day for six days with your armed men. Have seven priests carry trumpets of ram's horns in front of a gold box containing holy things, called the Ark of the Covenant of the Lord. On the seventh day, march around the city seven times with the priests blowing trumpets. After that, they will sound a long trumpet blast. Then have the people give a loud shout. The city walls will collapse, and the army will go straight in."

Joshua told the priests the battle plan that the Lord had given him. They brought the Ark out of the Tabernacle. Seven priests carried trumpets in front of it. Joshua ordered the army, "Advance and take up your weapons! March around the city. Go ahead of the Ark of the Covenant."

That's what they did. They walked around the city once a day for six days in a row. On the seventh day, they got up at dawn. They marched around the city seven times in a row. After the seventh time, the priests sounded the trumpets.

Joshua commanded the people, "Shout, for the Lord has given you this city! Jericho is to be destroyed. You may take anything from the city, except for the special things that belong to God. Remember, do not hurt Rahab or her family, because she helped the Israelites."

They shouted, then the walls of Jericho fell down. The soldiers charged in and took the city. Now the Israelites devoted this city to the Lord. God's power won the battle. This story about Joshua reminds us that, if God tells us how to do something, He wants us to do it His way. Jericho shows us God can win any fight.

Jericho Archaeological Site

****

Antique Lamp

Samuel talks to God

The story of Samuel actually starts with his mother. Her name was Hannah. She was married to a very good man, Elkanah. They both loved God, but Hannah was sad. She would cry, because she wanted to have a baby. She prayed and prayed. She asked God, "Please don't forget me. Please give me a child. If You give me a son, I will give him back to You. He will work for God, help the priests, and live in the Lord's presence forever."

Surprise—a miracle! Hannah had a baby boy, and they named him Samuel. Of course, Hannah and her husband kept their promise to send Samuel to work for God and help the priests. When he was a little bit older, they took him to the priest Eli, who was at Shiloh. They let him stay there and help Eli.

One night, the lamp of God was still burning. Samuel was sleeping in God's earthly house, the Tabernacle, which was a fancy tent built the way God wanted. All of a sudden, he heard a voice. The voice said, "Samuel!" Samuel woke up.

He ran to Eli. Samuel said, "Here I am. What do you want, Eli?"

Eli said, "I didn't say anything to you. It's time to rest."

So Samuel went to lie down, and then he fell asleep. Again, someone said, "Samuel!"

Samuel got up quickly. He went back to Eli, and said, "You called me?"

But Eli said, "No, I did not call you. Go to sleep. But if you notice the voice again, answer, 'Speak, Lord. Your servant hears.'"

Samuel said, "All right."

He went back to sleep and a little while later, he heard that same voice say, "Samuel!"

Samuel woke up and said, "I am here! Speak, Lord, for your servant is listening."

Do you know Whose voice that was? It was God. The Lord said, "I'm going to do something that will make everyone's ears tingle." God explained a part of His plan and added, "I will do all of it just as I said. You must tell people what I've told you."

God was asking Samuel to be His prophet, a special person who would listen to Him and do things for Him. Samuel said, "Yes, I will tell people what you ask me to say, Lord."

That's what Samuel did for his whole life. He listened to God. He shared with people what God told him. He led God's special people, the Israelites, for many years. Then Samuel anointed Saul, and they crowned him king to rule over Israel.

Samuel was a wonderful man, who loved the Lord from the time he was a little boy. So, God can even talk to little children. When He calls and they listen, they can share things God wants them to say.

Five Smooth Stones

David and Goliath

David was an Israelite. He was one of God's chosen people. Goliath belonged to another group called the Philistines. Now, the Philistines wanted to conquer, that means they wanted to take over another country. They hoped to come and take control of Israel. The Philistines and their army came to fight against the Israelites and their king named Saul. The two armies set up camps opposite each other so they could see and hear their enemies.

The Philistines' champion was named Goliath. He was enormous. He was a giant. Every day for forty days, he stood on the field between the two armies. He would say, "O people of Israel, you can't fight against us. I dare any one of your men to come and beat me! I will win if I fight any of you Israelites. If I win, you'll become our slaves." When the Israelites saw how huge Goliath was, they were afraid. Goliath was taunting, or saying bad things, to the Israelites.

Three of David's older brothers were in the army of King Saul. David wasn't there. One day, David's dad sent him to take some food to his brothers and their boss. When David came, he saw and heard Goliath saying terrible things about Israel. Goliath told everyone that the Philistines were going to conquer Israel and take over their land. Goliath said, "Your God can't help you against me. Look at me. I'm a giant!"

When David heard it, he said, "That is wrong. Who is Goliath to defy the Lord's army? God is greater than Goliath."

Now you know, David was too young to be in the army. He was a shepherd, which means he took care of his family's sheep. While he was watching the sheep, he had killed a lion and a bear. He knew that God was strengthening him to protect his father's sheep. David thought, *Since God helped me save the sheep, He will help me protect Israel by stopping Goliath.*

David told King Saul, "I will fight Goliath."

King Saul said, "O.K. I'll give you my armor and sword." They put King Saul's armor on David, but guess what? It was too big, because David was young and much smaller.

David said, "I can't wear this. It is just too heavy. I won't be able to do what I need to do." He took the armor off.

Instead of taking Saul's sword, David picked up five smooth stones, and he put them in the bag with his sling. I don't know if you've ever seen a sling. It's a leather strap. You put a stone in it, spin it around, and it shoots that rock at a high speed. David went to fight Goliath, who was a giant in thick armor with a sword and a shield. But here was David, just in his regular clothes, carrying five stones with his sling.

When Goliath saw David coming, he said, "Oh my goodness, this is all? You are sending this boy to fight me?"

Can you imagine what happened? David answered, "I come in the name of Israel's God. The whole earth will hear about the Lord of hosts. This battle belongs to God."

David ran toward him, took one of the stones, put it in his sling, and shot it. It hit Goliath right in the middle of his forehead, and he dropped over dead. After that, the Philistines ran away! David saved Israel. God gave him the power to win in a battle with a giant! This is another story about a young person who trusted God.

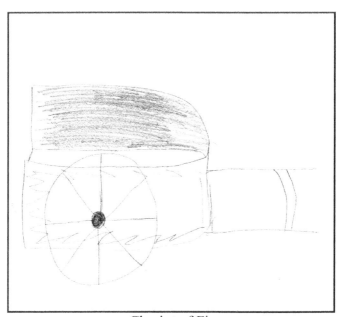
Chariot of Fire

Elijah and the Fiery Chariot

Elijah and Elisha were both prophets of the Lord. Do you know what a prophet is? It's someone who tells what's going to happen in the future. If everything a prophet said came true, the Israelites knew he was from the Lord. Elijah had been a prophet of the Lord for a long time. He'd been doing what God said and telling people what God wanted him to say. Elisha was his helper, doing anything that Elijah asked.

Elijah did many wonderful things. In God's power, he made a widow's supply of flour and oil last through a drought, raised a boy from the dead, and successfully prayed for rain.

The Lord showed Elijah that He would soon go up to heaven to be with Him. Elijah wasn't going to die like everybody else. The Lord was just going to bring him to heaven.

Elijah and Elisha were at Gilgal, which is a place in Israel. Elijah said, "God told me to go to Bethel. Won't you please stay here?"

But Elisha replied, "Not a chance. I won't let you go out of my sight. I won't leave you." He stayed right with Elijah. They went to Bethel.

When they arrived, there were other prophets who listened to the Lord. They came to tell Elisha, "Did you know that the Lord is going to call your master home forever today?"

"Yes, I know." Elisha said, "Shhh! Be quiet."

Then Elijah told Elisha, "Stay here. The Lord is sending me to Jericho."

But Elisha said, "As surely as the Lord lives, I won't leave you." So, they both went to Jericho.

Again, some prophets came out to tell Elisha, "Do you know that God is going to take your master, Elijah, from you today?"

"Yes, I know," answered Elisha. "So, please be quiet."

Then Elijah said to Elisha, "Please stay here. The Lord has sent me to the Jordan River."

But can you guess what Elisha said? "No way. As surely as you live, I won't leave you."

So the two men walked to the Jordan. When they got to the riverbank, Elijah took off his cloak, rolled it up, and hit the water with it. Have you heard what happened? The water divided to the right and to the left. Then the two of them went across on dry ground.

When they were on the other side, Elijah said to Elisha, "Tell me, what can I do for you before I am taken to heaven? Ask anything."

Elisha answered, "I want to be a holy man like you, but do twice as many miracles."

Elijah said, "You asked for a difficult thing. If you are watching when I'm taken from you, you'll get what you asked." As they were walking and talking together, suddenly a chariot of fire with fiery horses appeared, separating the two men.

Elijah went up to heaven in a whirlwind. Elisha saw him. Elisha shouted, "My father, my father—the chariots and horsemen of Israel!" Elisha didn't ever see him again. The Lord had taken Elijah up to heaven in the chariot.

Then Elisha went home, knowing that the Lord had given him the same Holy Spirit that Elijah had. What we remember from this story is that you can ask God for things. If what you ask is part of His plan for your life, He will give it to you at the right time. God always knows what you need. The important thing is to trust the Lord to decide what's best.

Wilderness of Judea, on a road to Jericho

Jonah's Big Fish

Jonah and the Big Fish

God came to a man called Jonah. He said, "Jonah, I want you to go to the people of Nineveh. Tell them that God loves them, but they need to stop doing evil things." Now, Jonah didn't like the people of Nineveh, because they did bad things all the time.

He thought to himself, *I don't want to do what God asked me.* Do you know what Jonah did? He stood up and got on a ship going away from Nineveh.

Suddenly there was a huge storm that went on and on. The ship's passengers and crew were afraid. They said, "Oh no, we're going to die!" While throwing things they didn't need into the sea, all the people were screaming, "Oh dear, what's going to happen?"

Have you heard what Jonah was doing? He wasn't worried at all. He was sleeping down inside the ship.

The captain woke up Jonah. He said to him, "How can you sleep? Pray to your God!"

Jonah said, "I know why we're in the storm."

The captain said, "Tell us. Why?"

"God asked me to do something for Him, but I didn't feel like doing it," Jonah said. "So, I ran the other way. If you want the storm to stop, throw me into the water." They didn't want to do that, because it's a bad thing to throw someone overboard. But Jonah said, "No, just throw me in the water."

They were so afraid of dying in the storm that they threw Jonah overboard. Immediately, the storm stopped, and the water was calm. Where was Jonah? He was down deep in the water, under the sea.

Can you guess what God did? He made a huge fish come along. That fish swallowed Jonah. Then Jonah was inside this enormous fish.

When he was inside the fish's belly, Jonah prayed, "I know I didn't do what You wanted me to do, God. I am sorry that I ran the other way. You heard my prayer, Lord. You rescued me when the waters came over me. I will do what You want me to do, God. Please let me go tell the people of Nineveh that You love them and want everyone to stop doing evil things."

Three days later, a miracle happened! The big fish swam close to shore and spit Jonah out onto dry land. Jonah got up. He went to the city of Nineveh. It took three days to walk across the whole city.

Everywhere Jonah went, he called out very loudly, "The one true God, Who loves you, sent me to tell you something important. Nineveh will fall in forty days, unless you repent and stop doing evil things." He walked through the whole town.

Can you imagine what happened? All the people—from the king to every young person—prayed, "We are truly sorry. We promise to stop doing evil things. We are going to listen to You, God." The story ended happily. Jonah delivered the message that God had for the people of Nineveh. They lived, because they started obeying God. Jonah's story reminds us to obey God in every situation.

Lion

Daniel and the Lions

Daniel was another one of God's chosen people. When Daniel was a young man, a faraway country conquered Israel, which means they took charge of Israel. Their king, Nebuchadnezzar, took some of the smart, young Israelites back to his capital city of Babylon.

Daniel loved God, the eternal Lord who created everything. He lived a very good life. As he grew up, he served different kings as a trusted adviser. That means, when the king was wondering about something, he would ask Daniel what he should do. When Daniel was older, he was such a good adviser that King Darius listened to him all the time. Darius wanted to promote Daniel to watch over the whole kingdom.

Well, there were some other advisers who were jealous of Daniel, because the king liked him so much. They decided to get Daniel in trouble. They knew that Daniel always prayed every day. He went to the windows that faced Jerusalem in his upper room. He would kneel down and pray. These other men suggested a new law telling everyone they could only pray to the king for a whole month.

The next time Daniel went to pray, they sent men to arrest him. The jealous officials brought Daniel before the king. These officials said, "Daniel, you know the new rule. You're not allowed to pray to anyone but King Darius. You were praying to your God."

Daniel said, "Yes. I am always going to do that, because He is the only true God."

The officials said, "Daniel, because you disobeyed, you have to be thrown into the lions' den."

Lions are very scary. They can hurt people. Also, they didn't feed these lions for a while.

The king said, "Well, I have to do it, because it's my law. May God help you, Daniel." They threw Daniel into the den where the hungry lions were. He had to stay there all night.

The king was upset, because he liked Daniel very much. He stayed in his palace and thought, *Daniel's going to be hurt by the lions*. He didn't eat, and he couldn't sleep. But, as soon as the sun came up, King Darius went out to see Daniel. He went to the den. Darius asked, "Daniel, servant of the living God, are you safe?"

Daniel answered, "Yes, my God sent His angel to stay with me."

Darius had the stone rolled away—a miracle! Daniel was there, unharmed. The lions were still there, but Daniel was fine. The king was so happy. He had Daniel taken out of the cave. King Darius said, "I'm glad you're O.K. I know now that the living God of Daniel works miracles."

Daniel agreed, "My God protected me the whole time I was in the den. I thank God. He's the one true God. He can protect people—even from hungry lions."

Gifts from the Magi

Jesus' Birth

Jesus is a very unique person. He is God. He has always been. Remember when we talked about God creating everything? Jesus was there, but later Jesus did something truly special. He stopped being up in heaven with God the Father. He came down and became a human being like us.

Every year, we celebrate Jesus' birthday. Do you know when we remember that day? Christmas!

We celebrate the birth of Jesus because He came to be with us. Miraculously, Jesus was born to a young woman named Mary. Mary and her betrothed husband, Joseph, had to go be registered in the town of Bethlehem for a census, which means counting every person in the country.

When they got to Bethlehem, there wasn't any good place for them to rest. So they stayed in a stable with the animals. That's where Baby Jesus was born. Because Jesus is God, His birth was a miracle. Even though He was born in a stable, there were angels singing to celebrate His birth.

In fact, there were some shepherds who were watching their sheep not too far away from where Jesus was born. All of a sudden, they looked up in the sky. There were stars sparkling and angels singing. They were saying, "Glory to God!" The angels told the shepherds that the Christ Child had been born, so the shepherds went to find the baby. They were actually the first ones to go see Jesus.

And in a faraway country, there were some astronomers, people who study the stars. These astronomers are usually called Magi. When Jesus was born, God put a beautiful star up in the sky. The Magi, or wise men, knew this star was special. They heard a story that, if you follow this unusual star in the sky, you'll find someone born to be the great king.

So these men traveled to search for the One, Who would be the everlasting king and Who would save people. They found Baby Jesus and brought Him gifts. They gave Him myrrh, which was a very expensive perfume. They brought gold, which of course you know is worth a lot. And they gave Him frankincense, a precious oil. They brought gifts worthy of a newborn prince to Baby Jesus, because they knew that He would be the greatest king ever. He came to love and save all of us. Jesus was born to show us how much God loves us.

Church of St. Catherine's Cloister,
near the traditional Bethlehem site of the Nativity

The Holy Spirit as a Dove

Jesus' Baptism

When Jesus was all grown up, He started His ministry. His family's hometown was Nazareth in Galilee. He went around the country telling everyone how much God loves them.

One day, He walked to the Jordan River. There was a man by the riverside named John the Baptist. He was talking to people who hoped to know God better. Many of them promised to change and live the way God wanted.

John encouraged people to show they were sorry for bad things they had done by being baptized. First, they'd go under the water. When they came up, they would say, "Now I'm clean. My life will be different. I have decided to follow God."

Jesus found John baptizing people. John looked at Him and said, "This is the Lamb of God. This is the special Son of God."

Jesus said to John the Baptist, "I am here so you can baptize Me."

Then John said, "Please baptize me, Jesus. You never did anything wrong. I don't think I should baptize You. You're more important than I am."

But Jesus said, "You need to baptize me."

So John baptized Jesus. Suddenly, when Jesus came up out of the water, the heavens opened. Then the Spirit of God, or Holy Spirit, came down from heaven, looking like a dove. The Spirit landed on Jesus. Another special thing happened. They heard a voice from heaven saying, "This is My Son, whom I love, with Him I am well pleased."

Remember when we talked about God in the beginning at Creation? There's God the Father, God the Son or Jesus, and God the Holy Spirit. All three of them were together in this story when Jesus was baptized in the Jordan River. Jesus knew God the Father would be delighted if He got baptized to declare publicly He has always belonged to God. It's important for us to follow Jesus' example and live the way God wants.

Jordan River in the dry season

****

Water Jar with Wine

Jesus at Cana

Jesus' mother, Mary, was invited to a wedding in Cana. Jesus and His friends were also invited. They were having a wonderful time. This wedding party, like others in Jesus' country, would last for days.

After a while, they had no more wine for people to drink at the party. Jesus' mother, Mary, heard about this problem. She wanted to help. Do you know what Mary did? She went to her son and said, "Jesus, they don't have enough wine for the wedding feast."

Jesus responded, "Why are you saying this to Me? It's not My time yet."

Jesus' mother just looked at Him. Then she told the servants, who were standing close by, "Do anything He tells you."

Jesus saw six stone water jars. They were huge jars—several feet tall. Each one held twenty to thirty gallons. Jesus told the servants to fill all the jars with water. This was hard work, because they had to go to the well and bring the water back.

The servants filled those huge stone jars with water and told Jesus. They did what He asked. He said, "Now, take some of the liquid to the master of the banquet."

The banquet master was in charge of running the wedding, so the parents didn't have to worry about everything. The servant took a full cup to the master of the banquet. When he tasted it, he couldn't believe it. He said, "Everyone brings out the good wine first and then the cheaper wine after the guests have had plenty to drink. But you have saved the best until now."

Jesus had turned that water into wine. Not just any wine, but the very best wine that anyone had ever tasted. This was the first miracle of Jesus' ministry. He blessed the people at a wedding.

He took this opportunity to help others after He listened to His mother. He did it when His mom encouraged Him. It's a good idea to listen to your mother. Only one of the Ten Commandments includes a blessing: **"Honor your father and mother so that you may have a long life in the land that the LORD your God is giving you"** (Exodus 20:12, HCSB). Jesus did that, and so can we.

Two Fish

Jesus feeds the 5,000

Jesus continued His ministry. He walked around telling people about God. He told them how much God loves them and how God wants us to live. Jesus said that God wants us to love Him and love others. He had some special friends with Him, called disciples. He also did a lot of miracles. One of the miracles happened after Jesus was healing the sick who came to see Him in a big crowd.

Jesus had healed many in a very large group of people. It was getting late. His disciples, who helped Him a lot, said, "What are we going to do? It's time to eat dinner. All of these hungry people—many, many men, women, and children—are here with You. We don't have any food to give them. And there isn't enough money to buy something."

Then Jesus looked at His disciples and said, "Why don't you feed them?"

One disciple, whose name was Andrew, said, "Well, I'm not sure, Lord. But this little boy has a small lunch that his mom gave him. The boy said we can have it, if it would help." He had two fish and five loaves of barley bread.

Jesus held that little lunch and said, "Thank you very much." He looked up to heaven and said, "My Heavenly Father, please take this food and bless it to feed all of these people."

Can you guess what happened? It did. That little bit of food was enough to feed every person. They kept sharing it, and the bread never ran out. In fact, Jesus asked the disciples to gather all the uneaten food. There were twelve basketfuls of bread left over.

It was a miracle! Jesus changed a little bit of food into enough to feed thousands of people and still have leftovers. He blessed them with more food than they wanted. That's how God is. He can give us everything we need. And then He keeps on giving! He blesses us, just like God fed these people who spent time with Jesus.

Sea of Galilee

Disciples' Boat

Jesus walks on water

Jesus did so many things. No book is big enough to hold all the stories about Him. After Jesus fed the 5,000 people, they went home. He told His disciples to get into a boat and cross the Sea of Galilee.

Jesus said, "You go ahead to the other side. I'll come later." Jesus went and spent some time alone with God the Father. He prayed almost the entire night on a mountain.

The disciples were in the boat. It was dark. All of a sudden, there was a big storm on the sea. The waves were crashing. The disciples were all very afraid. They said, "Oh no, what's going to happen to us?"

When the disciples looked around, they thought they saw something. What could it be? It looked like it might be a person, but this Man was walking on the water in a storm. They realized Jesus was coming. He was walking on the water. They could hardly believe it, and they were scared.

Jesus said, "Don't be afraid. It's Me."

One of the disciples, whose name was Peter, looked up. He said, "If it's You, Jesus, I want to get out of the boat and be with You."

Jesus said, "All right, Peter. Come and walk on the water, too."

Peter stepped out of the boat. Did you remember that there was still a storm? The waves were crashing.

But Peter started walking on the water. He was looking at Jesus.

All of a sudden Peter realized, *I'm walking on the water!* He saw all the waves. The water was hitting him. He started looking down. Then he was afraid. He started sinking into the water. He looked up to Jesus and said, "Lord, help me!"

Jesus did. Soon, He and Peter were in the boat. The storm stopped. Jesus protected him and all the other disciples. So if you're ever in trouble, just keep your eyes on Jesus. He always wants to help. He is able to do that, because He is God.

Zacchaeus' Tree

Jesus and Zacchaeus

Jesus kept on doing His ministry. Jesus was telling everybody how much God loves them and how we need to love God. Jesus was going through the town of Jericho near the Jordan River.

There was a man who lived in that place named Zacchaeus. Now, Zacchaeus was a very short, rich man. He made his money by cheating people. He heard of Jesus. He said to himself, *I'd like to hear more about Jesus.*

Have you heard what Zacchaeus did when he learned Jesus was coming to his town? He climbed up in a tree, so he could see and hear Jesus better.

When Jesus walked into town, many people wanted to be near Him. Do you know what happened? Jesus came walking in, and there were people crowding all around Him. Everyone wanted to see Him. He was surrounded. When He came near the tree where Zacchaeus was, Jesus looked up and said, "Zacchaeus."

Zacchaeus was surprised, because he didn't even know Jesus could see him sitting up in the tree. And he didn't realize that Jesus knew his name. But Jesus said, "Zacchaeus, come down from the tree. I'm going to stay at your house today."

Zacchaeus was so, so happy. He climbed out of the tree. He took Jesus back to his house and was a very generous host. He also invited Jesus' disciples to the party. Probably some of Zacchaeus's own friends came, too.

Zacchaeus enjoyed spending time with Jesus. He decided to live the way God wanted, to stop cheating people, and to give back what he stole. His whole life changed that day. That's what Jesus does. He changes people's lives for the better. He makes people happy, just by being with Him.

Clouds

Jesus' Heavenly Home

Jesus' home is in heaven. Heaven is where God lives. Remember how God created everything? God is actually three Persons. As you've probably heard before, the Persons are God the Father, God the Son or Jesus, and God the Holy Spirit. After God created the world, God made Adam and Eve, the first man and the first woman. God spent time with Adam and Eve in the Garden of Eden.

Then something very sad happened. God told Adam and Eve there was one thing that they could not do, which was eat fruit from the tree of the knowledge of good and evil. It's so sad, because Adam and Eve decided to do that one bad thing. What they did broke their friendship with God. Adam and Eve had to leave the garden. They didn't get to walk with God on earth any more.

And because that friendship, or relationship, was broken, all these things happened. You've heard stories from the Old Testament about Adam, Eve, Noah, Abraham, Sarah, Moses, Joshua, Samuel, David, Elijah, Elisha, Jonah, and Daniel. You also listened to New Testament stories with Mary, Joseph, the Shepherds, the Magi, John the Baptist, Andrew, Peter, and Zacchaeus. Many of these stories have been about Jesus—who is God, God's Son. Jesus came to earth so He could make the relationship between God and people good again.

Jesus came to save people. He did all kinds of miracles to show divine power. He has taught us Who God is, how much God loves every person, and how we need to listen to the Lord. Jesus came down from heaven to heal people's relationships with God. Jesus had to suffer. He even gave up His physical life, so He could heal the relationship with every person who believes in Him.

All we have to do is trust Jesus, because He did the work. Jesus made it possible to have peace with God. We can have the gift of a good relationship with the Lord.

Jesus came to earth, He grew up, and He taught anybody who would listen. He has shown everybody what God is like. He died on the Cross and was buried. But He was only laid to rest for a short time. Three days after He died, He rose. He became alive again. And He is alive today.

Jesus wants everyone to accept His gift of a good relationship with God. All you have to do is believe in Him, be sorry for all the bad things you've done, and then ask Him to save you. We can be adopted into God's forever family and become His friends. We can be among God's special people who go to heaven.

To His close friends, Jesus explained, "I'm going away to be with My Father." Then one day, Jesus said, "The Holy Spirit will help you be My witnesses. I'll always be with you." He floated up on a cloud to be with His Father in heaven again. They call that His ascension. In the future, all the people who love Jesus will be in heaven with Him. Someday I'll be there, waiting for you.

Jesus is in heaven today. He will come back and bring all His friends to His heavenly home. He wants us to be together forever. He's up there. You can't see Him right now, but He watches us.

He listens to us and prays for us. You can talk to Him. He loves you so much! He wants you to be adopted into His family. If you ever need to talk to Him, He's right there. You can just speak out loud, or you can even talk in your mind. God is always listening.

For God so loved the world that He gave His one and only Son, that whoever believes in Him shall not perish but have eternal life. For God did not send His Son into the world to condemn the world, but to save the world through Him.
-John 3:16-17 (NIV)

Jerusalem's Old City, including a site
traditionally associated with Jesus' Ascension

****

Notes

****

Notes

****

Questions

****

Questions

****

Drawings

****

Drawings

****

Drawings

Bible References

Creation: Genesis 1, 2, and 3:8
Noah and the Flood: Genesis 6:9-9:17
Abraham and Baby Isaac: Genesis 11:27-31, 12:1-8,
       17:1-8, 17:15-21, 18:1-15, and 21:1-7
Moses and the Exodus: Exodus 1-3, 12:31-39, and
       14:1-31; Acts 7:20-34
Joshua and Jericho: Joshua 5:10-15 and 6
Samuel talks to God: I Samuel 1 and 3
David and Goliath: I Samuel 17
Elijah and the Fiery Chariot: I Kings 17:8-24 and
       18:41-45; II Kings 2:1-15
Jonah and the Big Fish: Jonah 1-3 and 4:2
Daniel and the Lions: Daniel 1 and 6
Jesus' Birth: Matthew 2:1-12 and Luke 2:1-20
Jesus' Baptism: Matthew 3:13-17; Mark 1:9-11;
       Luke 3:21-22; John 1:29-34
Jesus at Cana: John 2:1-11
Jesus feeds the 5,000: Matthew 14:13-21 and
       John 6:1-14
Jesus walks on water: Matthew 14:22-33 and
       John 20:30-31
Jesus and Zacchaeus: Luke 19:1-10
Jesus' Heavenly Home: Genesis 2:16-24 and 3;
       Matthew 28:16-20; Mark 16:19-20;
       John 20:17; Acts 1:7-11; Romans 6:23;
       Hebrews 7:25; I John 1:9